Timeless Copywriting Secrets

15 Secrets For Writing More
Persuasive And Profitable Words
Better Than Anyone You Could Hire

Fraser Druet

ISBN: 978-1-9995771-1-7

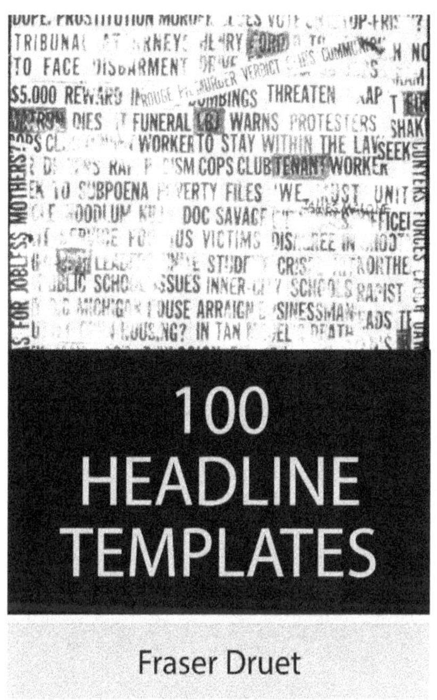

READ THIS FIRST

As a way of saying thank you for buying my book, here is a link to my '**100 Headline Templates**' Ebook 100% FREE!

It contains 100 simple ideas and corresponding examples you could incorporate into your headlines. Try incorporating some and test them to see which ones your market responds best to.

TO DOWNLOAD GO TO:

https://FraserDruet.com/BookDownloadBonus

This book is dedicated to the top 5%. Those who actually finish what they set out to accomplish. Those who do whatever it takes.

TABLE OF CONTENTS

CHAPTER ONE

Introduction

Dear Friend,

My name is Fraser Druet and I'm going to show you how to write powerful sales material that gets people to convert better online and offline.

I've spent the last five years growing my marketing business and copywriting ability. I've gone from a novice who wrote affiliate-marketing articles few wanted to click on. Now I've run lead-generation campaigns that have given some clients up to 97 times return-on-investment in ad-spend.

At first, I wasted MONTHS of my time when I tried to learn how to write effective copy ('copy' is a marketing industry term for "persuasive writing"). That's because I was consuming generic and useless blog articles, podcasts, YouTube videos, and books from popular 'gurus.'

This made me discouraged with the modern 'teachers' of

copywriting. I then turned to the past to find selling ideas that have been in use for over a hundred years.

I came across copywriting greats such as Joe Sugarman and David Ogilvy. Then I hit the motherlode and found the greatest copywriter of his time: Gary Halbert. It was through reading his "Boron Letters" book and some of his old newsletters that I stumbled upon his copywriting challenge.

His challenge promised a way to become "a better copywriter than anyone you could hire" in only 30 days. I basically just had to read a bunch of copywriting books and hand-copy a bunch of proven ads and headlines. Or so I thought...

I cut through all the modern marketing B.S. to develop tested and timeless sales skills. Skills I could use to help clients, and also cost-effectively test, promote, and sell my own products.

Nine months and one week later, I'd finished the Gary Halbert challenge. Better late than never. Though at the same time I came to learn I might be the only person to complete the challenge in one dedicated sitting, as prescribed by Gary.

Other legendary copywriters have read the same books and done similar exercises, but over a period of years.

In fact, Dan Kennedy, one of the greatest living copywriters and marketers, related a conversation he had with the late Gary Halbert.

Gary had always recommended hand-copying proven ads and headlines. He said it was one of the best exercises people could do to improve their copywriting abilities. He estimated he gave this advice to 10,000 to 15,000 people at his seminars and other venues. Though Gary thought maybe about five people actually did it.

From Dan's own experience, he estimated around 12 people did it from his similar recommendations over the years.

Again, these are the most highly-recommended exercises you could do. Especially to improve your copywriting skills. They were prescribed from the greatest modern copywriters, as well as many legendary copywriters from the past.

So I found I was in a very exclusive group… which leads us to this book.

Now, who's this book for? It's for someone who does any online or offline writing, advertising, or marketing.

It's even for people who're primarily on social media, since social media is largely about making people take the next step down your sales funnel.

With that in mind, it's probably a good idea for you to master the ability to craft converting sales copy as quickly, easily, and powerfully as possible.

I'll guide you through the great copywriting lessons I've harvested from the recommended copywriting books from Gary Halbert. And I'll include more online-oriented strategies as well.

So, who shouldn't read this book? If you're someone who doesn't want to write "salesy" copy…

If you want people to read your headlines and think "that's clever/'well-written'/funny/beautiful/cutesy/entertaining/etc" then you should put down this book. Then you can learn what it feels like to write material where few people read past the headline (if they notice it at all), let alone take any action.

I'm going to take you through the top copywriting guidelines, ideas, and exercises. Expert copywriters have used them for over 100 years (and they'll still be effective 100 years from now).

Let's build up your copywriting ability to the point where you can sell with words better than anyone you could hire.

Onward!

CHAPTER TWO

What are the core most powerful and most converting copywriting methods to leverage?

Before you type a single word of copy, there are three tasks even more important you must complete. You must first find the most profitable market. Then you should figure out if the arithmetic works for that market. And you should research the heck out of what you've decided to sell to that hot market.

Only once you complete these three tasks can you focus on the four most powerful parts of selling with the written word. They are:

- Benefits
- Proof
- Headline
- Bullets

If you can nail these four areas, you'll be nailing at least

95% of the selling power of your ads. I will be covering all of the above in the following chapters.

Are you ready?

CHAPTER THREE

Why is picking the most profitable market important?

Well, for the answer, let's look to who was considered to be the greatest copywriter of his time, Gary Halbert.

He used to give people at his seminars this example. Suppose you had a hot dog sales stand and your goal was to make the most money from it. You could also have any advantage you wanted to help you sell hot dogs. Gary wanted only one advantage. And he believed his advantage would beat the combined advantages of all the ideas his seminar students would give him.

People would think they should have the best product. Gary would say no, my advantage still beats that.

Next, they'd say having a great location is the most important advantage. Nope.

Maybe it's having side orders? Maybe it's having good

drinks? Using the locally-sourced organic ingredients? Having a good advertising campaign? Coverage on TV? No, no, no!

Gary would say "you can have all of those combined, and I'll still beat you." Because Gary would say the only advantage he'd want... is a starving crowd.

Taking a step back, that's how you should look at your business.

You want to find the hungriest market. So you don't necessarily need the best product. If there's not a hungry market for your product, then you're not going to make money and you're not going to help anyone.

So take a step back and make sure what you're selling has a hungry market of people that want to buy it.

That's rule number one.

And we haven't even talked about traditional copywriting topics like the headline or what to write.

That's not important right now, because they won't matter if you're not writing to a hungry market. You could have the best headline, the best copy, the best proof elements, some legitimately great benefits, and so on...

But if nobody wants what you're selling... if there's not a market for it, then it doesn't matter. None of those things will matter. So that's why we want to get the foundations right up front.

Now, how can you identify your most profitable market or any hungry market to test?

Well, you find out what is selling now.

Your first job is to find a market to sell to. And how do

you find these markets? Well, a good rule of thumb is to find out what is already selling.

Check out the Amazon bestseller lists. Not only for books, but for all sorts of electronic consumer products and even some services.

See what is trending on Google Trends.

Also, check out some lists on Nextmark of what people have bought. This is currently a free service.

Want another good indicator a market is hot? Find out if there's a magazine dedicated to your market niche. Is your market popular enough and passionate enough that people have created and dedicated a magazine to it? For example, there are many golfing magazines, because the golfing market is hot.

But do you notice there are not a lot of ping-pong magazines and North America? That's because there's not a hungry market for ping-pong in North America right now.

One secret hint few know about is using the SRDS (Standard Rate & Data Service). You can pay for access to the SRDS Direct Marketing List Source for a more extensive list of what people have bought. You can find out what the product is, how many people bought it, how much they paid for it on average, and so on.

And when you multiply how many people bought a product by its average unit of sale, you can get an idea of the purchasing power of a particular market. That's powerful knowledge to have.

Now, don't feel you're stuck if this is a shocking revelation for you. You may have realized you have no market or a very limited market for what you're selling. If that's the case, don't feel bad. This happens to a lot of people.

Instead, you should feel happy you figured this out. Now you won't waste more months or years trying to sell to a cold or small group of people. Many business owners make this mistake, and many more will never figure it out.

So if you have figured out you need to find a bigger and hotter market, you have multiple options. You can find a more relevant and passionate market in your niche and tweak your products to fit that niche.

If your market's hopeless, then don't feel bad. Switch to another one. Find one that has a big group full of hungry, passionate, and wealthy prospects.

Next, how can you identify their demographics?

One way to identify the demographics of your market is to use Facebook Audience Insights.

Go onto Facebook Business Manager. If you haven't signed up yet, sign up for Facebook Business Manager to create a business account on Facebook.

Then you can use something called Audience Insights. You enter in interests and you can find related interests. So if you're marketing to golfers and one of the interests is golf, you can see a whole bunch of related interests to get an idea of who these people are. It helps you find what else are they're interested in.

It'll help you get answers to questions like "Who are these people? What is the breakdown of the interests they like? What percentage of golfers like each interest? And also how does it break down by age/sex/location/etc?"

You'll get these demographic and psychographic data

points from Facebook Audience Insights. I recommend using it to help you figure out your hungry market.

CHAPTER FOUR

What is the "arithmetic" and why is it important?

Okay, so now you've figured out your most profitable market.

Next is figuring out how profitable it could be.

You might be thinking "wait, we still haven't even touched anything to do with an actual advertisement."

Of course not.

Before we advertise, we want to make sure we can actually make money with it.

That's why we're talking about the arithmetic.

Some say the arithmetic is calculating how profitable a market can be.

To calculate the arithmetic, you first need to figure out your average lifetime customer value (LTV). LTV is how much money on average a customer will give your business over their lifetime.

It's not always an easy number to estimate, because it's always changing. You can get a good initial estimate by dividing your total profit over the years by the number of customers you've served. I hope you've been keeping track of repeat customers to make this estimate more accurate.

Try to be aware your LTV changes as you introduce new products and services over the years, and also change price points among other variables.

If you are unsure of your LTV, because you are still researching your market, then it becomes a little more difficult. You'll have to reach out to enough business owners in that niche to get an accurate answer. This also applies to the next calculation you'll need.

Next, you'll need to figure out how much on average it costs to get a customer. You can calculate this by taking your advertising costs, say, over the previous year. Then divide it by the number of new customers you got during the same period (including referrals).

Now, when you know both your LTV and how much it costs on average to get a new customer, you'll know if your business is profitable. If it costs more to get a new customer than the LTV, then you know this business isn't profitable.

If it is profitable, then you can get a good estimate of how profitable it can be by subtracting the average cost to get a new customer from the LTV. Then multiply that by the average number of new customers you get each month to have a good estimate of your potential monthly net income.

Again, this is only a rough estimate. Though it's an important one.

There's a more important point here. As long as you know

how much on average a customer brings in over their lifetime, you know how much you can spend to get a new customer.

So if your average lifetime customer value was $100, for instance, then you could spend up to $100 to get a customer and still be profitable. Remember, LTV is net profit over their lifetime after expenses.

You'd be able to spend up to $100 on advertising to get a single customer.

Now, if your average lifetime customer value was $1,000, then you could spend up to $1,000 to get a customer. That extra money to work with would mean you could advertise in more competitive markets. You could advertise in more competitive magazines, websites, direct mail, and email lists to get a customer.

You could even spend a lot more to get referrals. People would be happy to refer everyone they knew for hundreds of dollars in cash or other referral bonuses.

A high LTV gives you more options. Though it's different for every industry, market, product, and business.

One secret is if your LTV was $100, you'd much rather advertise in cheaper mediums. You'd rather pay $10 to advertise to get a customer than use mediums where it'd cost $80 to get a customer.

Where a lot of people go wrong is when they try to advertise exclusively in the mediums with the lowest cost per customer.

But this is wrong.

What you should try to do is maximize the amount of

money you spend in each medium, maxing it out. Start with the most profitable mediums to max out, then work your way down to the least profitable (but still profitable) mediums.

Don't discount other mediums because they're more expensive.

As long as you're making a profit, you should spend as much money as possible in each medium. So first, you max out your advertising spend in the medium that costs $10 to get a customer. Next, you max out the second cheapest medium, then the third. And so on. All the way until you reach an advertising medium that isn't profitable.

For example, you can start with maxing out adspend on Facebook, then max it out on Google ads, then email lists, then direct mail, and so on. Of course, that's only an example of the order your business might use. The order you'd use is different for every market. Some of those mediums aren't profitable at all for certain markets. You'll have to test and find out.

In conclusion, keep spending until you max out each advertising medium, from the most profitable, to the least profitable.

That's how you do it.

This way, you will maximize the amount of income you get.

Again, you don't want to minimize your advertising costs. You want to maximize your profits. Always stay focused on maximizing profits and you will do very well.

CHAPTER FIVE

Why is research the most valuable part of copywriting?

Most of the great copywriters, including Gene Schwartz, Gary Halbert, and Gary Bencivenga, all agree on the value of research.

After you get the market selection and arithmetic correct, you should focus on doing more research. Dig deeper than your competitors.

Research is the foundation of all great copy.

Why is that? It's because the more you research... The deeper you dig... The more nuggets of 'gold' you'll dig up,

For example, let's say you're selling a book for a doctor. You'll want to know more about the book you're selling than the doctor who wrote the book. If you've researched that much, then you'll be able to find benefits and unique facts in the book. The book's target market would love to know about them. And why limit yourself to one or two major benefits, when you can dig up all the valuable benefits the readers will get.

Why is that important? Well, some people in your market don't buy a product because of the major benefits the product brings.

In fact, some people might be persuaded to buy the book from only one benefit from a list of dozens. Though you must keep in mind you have no way of knowing which of these dozens of benefits will convert which prospect.

That's why it's great to include ALL of the benefits you've dug up in your copy. A common way of incorporating them is via lists of 'bullets,' which we'll discuss more in a later chapter.

But won't that long list make their eyes glaze over and stop reading? It would... for someone outside of your market. For someone who these benefits aren't relevant to.

But for your target market, these product benefits will deeply resonate with them. And for them, your promotion can't be too long, only too boring & irrelevant.

This is the long-tested concept of 'long copy.' From testing over the years, long copy has consistently increased sales. The longer it is, the more sales it produces, as long as each sentence is relevant to the target reader.

Another aspect of extensive research is 'creativity.'

Gene Schwartz used to say there is no such thing as creativity since nothing is created out of nothing.

Instead, he believed in 'connectivity.' He believed different ideas connect together to make something new and valuable.

When you research well, you generate extensive lists of benefits, proofs, and specific facts about your product. And when you educate yourself on copywriting, you learn about hundreds of effective selling-ideas. Ideas that have sold throughout the years. Ideas that don't change, because human nature doesn't change.

The true power of copywriting is connecting these lists of researched gold nuggets with your hundreds of selling ideas. They will help you craft hard-hitting promotions that will convert every prospect who is convertible.

That's why Gene liked to call it 'connectivity.'

So you should dedicate as much time as you need to dig up proof, benefits, features, and specifics claims about your product. The more of them you can dig up, the more of them you can connect with selling ideas to create killer advertising.

That's the value of research.

The more you can dig up, the more you have to work with. And the more powerful you can make your promotions, the more money you'll make.

Research is also the ultimate cure for writer's block.

The great copywriter Gary Bencivenga once wrote in a Marketing Bullets article of his "I learned that good copywriters get to know so much about the product and the prospect and his or her wants, fears, assumptions, and lingo that the copy soon wants to burst forth as if a dam is breaking. I learned that research is the infallible cure for writer's block."

Here's one last bonus benefit of extensive research. The more of these benefits you dig up and list, the more valuable your product will appear to your prospects, and thus, the more they'd be willing to pay for it.

CHAPTER SIX

Why are benefits important?

First of all, what are benefits?

Well, for example, if you were advertising a car, and the headline said '420 horsepower.' Well, that's not a benefit when you think about it.

That's a 'feature.'

It's a specific feature of the car. It has an engine that produces 420 horsepower. Now, that feature by itself doesn't actually help you. If you take a step back, you'll realize having a powerful engine by itself isn't beneficial. It's what that powerful engine can do for you that makes it valuable.

That's what matters.

The real benefits are the beneficial applications of features.

So in this case, if you're going to write a benefit, you wouldn't write "420 horsepower." You'd want to write something like "It takes you from zero to sixty miles per hour in only 4.6 seconds, which is faster than any car in its price category."

Now, that's the benefit!

The specific benefit of that powerful engine is you can accelerate very quickly relative to similarly priced cars. So that's a good example of the benefit.

And that's what motivates people to buy. Mere features don't generate the same level of appeal or sales power.

Give them an answer to their question "what can this product do for me?"

People still like to know the features, but ideally in the form of specific proofs. A way of going deeper into the benefits. An example of incorporating a feature as a proof element is "it takes you from zero to sixty miles per hour in just 4.6 seconds, which is faster than any car in its price category, because it has a 420 horsepower engine."

Now, that's a valid use of features. Because it's a very specific feature. It makes it more believable as a proof element. That's a good way to use features.

Now, going even deeper, there are also 'benefits of benefits.'

An example of this would be if the benefit is "it takes you from zero to sixty miles per hour in just 4.6 seconds, which is faster than any car in its price category." Then the benefit of this benefit might be "it makes all the other car drivers in your price category jealous that you can accelerate more quickly than them. And you can impress people more than in a slower car."

That's the benefit of the benefit.

And if you think about it, you could actually go even deeper than that... by asking "what does that get you?" Then "what does THAT get you?" And so on... Though we don't have to go there right now.

I'm sure you can imagine applying this deep line of questioning to your own products.

How do benefits both show and justify the value of what people are buying?

Benefits help illustrate the true value of what people are purchasing.

By adding more benefits to your promotions, it helps justify the value of your product to people and make them feel justified in paying more for it.

So in general, the more benefits you add, the more you can justify higher prices. That's because you're proving your product is that valuable to them.

CHAPTER SEVEN

Why is proof important?

Proof helps people believe what you're saying about your product is true.

You can list all the benefits in the world and people still won't buy if they don't believe what you're saying is true or real. They won't buy if they think you're making it up or embellishing.

Give them concrete proof to back up each of the benefits, then people will be more happy to buy to get those benefits when they actually believe them.

What are the various types of proof? You can find a lot of the different types in the book 'How to Write a Good Advertisement,' written by Victor Schwab.

He wrote an elaborate list of all the different types of proof, such as:

- Construction evidence

- Reputation and standing of your company

- Management personnel

- Production or service personnel

- Quality of materials or design

- Patents or machinery

- Speed of delivery

- Design or material of container

- Performance evidence

- Achievements of product

- Discriminating or well-known users

- Increasing popularity

- "Demonstration" reasons

- Testimony of others

- Expert evidence

- Awards or contests won

- Significant outlets selling product successfully

- Test evidence

- A strong guarantee

- Free sample

As you can see, there are many different types of proof elements. And those are only the major ones listed by Victor. I still recommend you buy that book to find more elaborate details of each.

Can you inject too much proof into your copy?

You almost can't, as long as the proof is relevant to your target market. They won't find relevant proof boring.

The more proof, the better.

You can't go wrong with saturating your product promotion with as much proof as possible.

Next, why is demonstration one of the most powerful forms of proof?

The great copywriter Claude Hopkins once said, "no argument in the world can ever compare with one dramatic demonstration."

Gary Bencivenga referenced an interesting demonstration in his farewell seminar. The Otis elevator demonstration was an example of how powerful demonstrations can be as proof.

Back in the 1800s when elevators first came out, there was fear of elevator cables snapping and people plummeting to their deaths.

A lot of people were wary of them, so that's why there weren't a lot of tall buildings back then. Because to have a tall building, you need safe and functional elevators. But if people don't want to ride, because they're skeptical of elevators, then nobody's going to construct tall buildings.

That was until a man named Elisha Otis came along to demonstrate his new elevator safety device to people at the World's Fair of the year 1854. This safety device for elevators would automatically secure and lock the elevator into place in the event of the cable snapping.

Initially, as great as it sounded, people were skeptical.

That was until he demonstrated his device in action at the World's Fair.

In front of crowds, he would tie a rope to an exposed

elevator equipped with his device. He'd then raise this elevator a few stories using a crane. When the demonstration started, he'd be on top of the elevator someone above him with an axe. And he'd let people know the rope was going to be chopped. He claimed his device would immediately snap into place and everything would be safe. There'd be no risk of injury.

People were very skeptical of course, because they hadn't believed before. His demonstrations drew large crowds.

When the time came the rope was hit with the axe. The rope snapped and the elevator dropped a very short distance as it locked securely into place. Then from that moment on the public believed elevators could be safe.

Fig. 1. Elisha Otis demonstrating his elevator safety hoist, Crytsal Palace, 1854. Image Credit: Wikimedia Commons

That's why there are tall buildings being constructed to this day.

A single demonstration made the perception of elevators to the public go from being a deathtrap to something safe. That's the power of demonstration.

For another more modern example of using an effective demonstration as powerful proof, check out this video ad by Purple Mattress. It's titled "How to Use a Raw Egg to Determine if Your Mattress is Awful - Purple Mattress" and can be watched here: https://youtu.be/4BvwpjaGZCQ

That mattress ad uses many powerful copywriting ideas. And at the heart of them is one very powerful and convincing demonstration of this mattress. It's demonstrated to be so soft that even 1400 lbs on top of a glass sheet cannot crush the four raw eggs between the glass sheet and the mattress. While the competition's mattresses all crush the eggs in their respective demonstrations.

Try to find a way to incorporate demonstration or stunts into your promotion if you can. Though still use every other type of proof available to you.

The more relevant proof you can inject into your advertising, the better.

CHAPTER EIGHT

Why is the headline important?

The headline might be the most important part of a promotion.

This is because the headline can be responsible for up to 95% or even more of the success of your promotion. That's what John Caples found when he tested various headlines for one of his sales promotions. The winning headline out-pulled the worst-performing headline by 19 times.

Not 19 percent more sales, but 19 TIMES more sales!

A great headline can MULTIPLY the effectiveness of your promotion.

Taking a step back, you have to wonder what the purpose of the headline is.

What is the ultimate purpose of the headline?

To start, let's talk about what the headline's purpose is NOT to do. It's not to entertain. It's not to be clever. Not to be cutesy, funny, 'well-written,' beautiful, profound, etc.

The headline's only job is to get noticed and make your target prospect want to read further or take the next step.

If the next step is to read the next line below the headline, then that's what the headline must help accomplish.

Let's go back to John Caples' 19x headline example. The losing promotion lost because people either didn't notice it or they weren't motivated enough by it to read further. Remember, the rest of the words in the promotion were the same. It was only the power of the winning headline which motivated people to actually read the rest of the promotion.

So what are some quick formulas and guidelines to help craft more converting headlines?

Here's a quick list of guidelines I've copied from my headlines book. Try to apply as many as you can to your headlines as you craft them.

1.   Make your headline target your reader's Self-Interest. What's in it for them?

2.   Make your headline Newsworthy or Buzzworthy

3.   Arouse Curiosity in your headline

4.   Inject HYPER-Curiosity by pairing curiosity with current celebrities/authorities/trends/events/etc in your headline

5.   Make your headline's solution sound quick & easy, yet believable

6.   Be as specific as possible in your headline

7.   Don't try to call attention to the headline itself (People shouldn't notice the words. The words should be like a clear window showing your

attractive product on the other side. If they notice the words and not the product, then your window is dirty)

8. The only purpose of the headline is to capture the attention of your target market, and make them want to read further or take the next step in the sales process

9. Write out 25+ headline variations, using proven headlines for inspiration when applicable

10. Test the best ones to find the winner

Sound good?

CHAPTER NINE

What are some ways to become a better headline-writer?

The best way to write great headlines... is to write great headlines.

Now, what the heck does that mean?

Isn't that a paradox?

The answer is no. The best way to learn is by hand-copying great headlines from the past. Proven headlines, which sold their respective products very profitably and effectively.

You can find a great compilation of proven headlines in the book '2001 Greatest Headlines Ever Written.'

From traditional publications, you can find great headlines in the cover blurbs of the National Enquirer and Cosmopolitan magazines.

You can also search online to find compilations of the

most clicked headlines from sites like BuzzFeed, ViralNova, and Upworthy.

Many of the best copywriters of all time recommend hand-copying headlines and whole ads. They have done so themselves.

Hand-copying great headlines gives you a feel for what it's like to write great headlines. A good analogy for this is great painters in the past would trace the masterworks of the great painters before them. That's how they became better painters.

The same technique is used to write novels. Hunter S. Thompson and Jack London were best-selling authors who did this. They hand-copied (by typewriter in Hunter's case) great novels to prime their own writing efforts.

In the movie industry, the great Japanese director Akira Kurosawa practiced it. He would encourage aspiring directors to hand-copy successful screenplays.

This concept works in all of those industries. And it works just as well for copywriting.

Start by hand-copying headlines and cover blurbs from the sources I gave. These are also sources Gary Halbert recommended people hand-copy from.

Then when you feel brave enough, you can hand-copy some full-blown sales letters.

CHAPTER TEN

Why are bullets important?

Bullets are condensed selling points of your product. Try to combine them with proof to back up their claims.

There are various types of bullets:

- Benefits your product offers

- Proof elements of your product

- Facts or claims about your product

They are usually preceded by an asterisk, dot, dash, or number in the case of a numbered list of bullets.

The most effective version of a bullet is a benefit your product offers combined with proof to back it up.

Your product might have many different benefits your market might want.

Out of dozens of bullets in your promotion, there might only be a single bullet a prospect will resonate with enough to make them buy.

That's why it's great to have more bullets. Dig up more benefits, proof elements, and specific facts & claims via research. The more bullets you put into your promotion, the more people you'll convert.

A side effect of having more bullets is the more bullets you have showing the value of your product, the more valuable your product appears to be. And thus, you can justify higher prices with more bullets.

That's because you're justifying the value. You're listing all the different ways your product delivers value to your target market.

Now, what's a good way to harvest bullets from your product? Gary Halbert had a recommended way.

He recommended you record your top salesman or yourself selling your product on the phone in peak state to your prospect. Then have the most effective sales presentation transcribed, and then make a total of three copies of that transcript.

First, go through one transcript line-by-line, and highlight all the different benefits of your product. Then write each benefit on an index card.

In the next transcript, highlight each proof element you find. Then write each proof element on an index card.

Then read through your third transcript while highlighting all the specific facts and claims of your product. Then write each fact & claim on an index card.

You should have three piles of index cards. Use these index cards to help craft bullets. And you can also use them to form the structure of your promotion as well.

It's an effective way of digging up and crafting bullets.

CHAPTER ELEVEN

What's the lead and why is it important?

The lead is a combination of the headline and the first few hundred words of your copy.

The lead is what draws people into your promotion. So by the time they're done reading the lead, they're hooked and want to read the rest.

That's the purpose of the lead. It's what hooks people into your copy to read further. That should be the job of it.

Every single sentence in your copy should make readers want to read the next sentence. That's the entire job.

Some people even think mountains of bullets aren't even necessary if you have a good enough lead. Of course, the answer in this case, as in every other case in copywriting, is to TEST everything to find the true answer. Or why not develop and include both?

The mountain of bullets should win. But hey, it's always worth testing. If someone thinks they've found something valuable, go ahead and test it.

That brings us next to the idea of 'long copy.'

CHAPTER TWELVE

How long should your copy be?

There's an overused expression applied to copywriting from Abe Lincoln that goes "How long should your legs be? Long enough to reach the ground."

It gets the message across, but we can do better. A better answer is your copy can never be too long, only too boring.

Your target market will read anything as long as it's relevant and interesting to them. Promotions of over 100 pages have out-pulled shorter promotions.

Of course, this all depends on your product. For example, there's only so much you can write about a box of paperclips if that's what you're selling.

Long copy also illustrates the value of deep and exhaustive research. The more value you can dig up about your product, the longer you can write your copy, and the higher your conversion rate will be.

There's a great story from Victor Schwab's book 'How to

Write a Good Advertisement' that helps illustrate the rule and validity of long copy. It involved the major advertiser Max Hart, and his advertising manager, George L. Dyer.

They were arguing about long copy. To prove its value, George said "I'll bet you $10 I can write a newspaper page of solid type and you'd read every word of it."

Max was skeptical. "I don't have to write a line of it to prove my point," George responded. "I'll only tell you the headline. That would be "This Page is all about Max Hart!""

As long as you can keep it interesting and relevant to your prospect, the longer your copy is, the more it'll sell. As illustrated by that story, people will read any amount of copy, so long as it's all relevant to them.

That's the general rule about long copy.

Next, we'll discuss some modern limitations of long copy with online platforms that have character limits and space limits.

CHAPTER THIRTEEN

How can you master copywriting online where

there are size and character limits?

You apply multiple steps to your promotion.

First, write out your long sales promotion. Then condense it into a headline that fits the limitations of your online advertising platform. Then use that medium as the first step of your sales funnel, which directs prospects to your long form sales copy on your landing page. Or to wherever your next step is.

You can only write so much on these platforms. Though at the same time, your copy can still be 'long' by incorporating multiple steps. For example, a one-line Google ad can still lead to a 100-page sales page. You'll have to condense and test the various headlines and appeals to drive people to that page.

So long copy still works with modern advertising platforms. There are just more steps involved. So don't worry about it.

Work within the character limits as you condense your core sales message as much as possible to fit within the limits. Then use that first step to direct your prospects to mediums where you have unlimited space, words, opportunities, and additional steps to sell them.

CHAPTER FOURTEEN

What's the difference between good and bad advertising?

The difference between good and bad advertising is quite simple.

There's an easy way to illustrate it.

Have you ever read an advertisement where you thought "wow, this advertisement is very clever/entertaining/cutesy/well-written/profound/beautiful/etc" and maybe you even wanted to share it with a friend?

If you've seen something like that, then you've seen an example of bad advertising.

Now, this is counter-intuitive to what most of the public (and most of the advertising industry) believe. But I'll illustrate to you right now why this is so.

Have you ever read anything, an article or news story or advertisement or something that when you read it, your attention was captured and you had to act? Where you had to click the buy button, dial the number, get in your car and drive to a store to buy it immediately, or somehow take action right away?

If you've read something like that, you've read an example of good advertising.

Good advertising gets people to buy. Bad advertising doesn't. It's as simple as that.

And that's the best way to think about it.

Legendary advertiser David Ogilvy once said "If you spend your advertising budget entertaining the consumer, you're a bloody fool. Homemakers don't buy a new detergent because the manufacturer told a joke on television last night. They buy the new detergent because it promises a benefit."

Going deeper, another way to think about it is to picture your advertisement as a storefront window. Then picture your product or service displayed behind the glass.

The window itself should have the clearest glass possible. That lets your target market see through the window to see the benefits of your product on display. They should see their desire or problem and how your product can help get them what they want.

But if the window is dirty... If the window tries to draw attention to itself... Then that's all your prospect will notice.

That's why you should strive to make your advertising like a clear window displaying the benefits of your product.

Show how your product can help them.

You shouldn't try to draw attention to the advertisement

itself.

That is the example of good and bad advertising Gene Schwartz gave in his Roedale presentation.

And one good thing to keep in mind when writing copy is it shouldn't try to be clever, funny, profound, or cutesy. Instead, the writing itself should be clear and easy to read.

That's it.

Don't think you have to adjust the reading level for how educated your market it. Rocket scientists and brain surgeons want to read clear and easy to read copy as much as ditch-diggers do. So keep your copy as clear and easy to read as possible.

Guide your reader through your product while drawing all the conclusions for them.

Don't expect your reader to come to the conclusions on their own. You should always be explicit when you're describing your product and how it can help them every step of the way.

Don't even assume the rocket scientists will draw conclusions about how your product can help them. You should hold their hand and try to 'do the thinking for your reader' every step of the way.

You'll want to write as clear and easy to read as possible. No matter who you're writing to.

And do the thinking for them.

Draw the conclusions for them.

CHAPTER FIFTEEN

How can you become a better copywriter?

Well, the late and great Gary Halbert... The "prince of print"... Who was considered by many to be one of the greatest copywriters of his era...

He once gave an answer to that question in the form of a 30-day copywriting challenge of his own design. It had the target goal of making someone a better copywriter than "anyone they could hire."

The challenge was broken up into the following steps:

1. Read eight classic copywriting books plus all of Gary's copywriting newsletters

2. Hand-copy nine successful sales letters

3. Reread those eight books & newsletters, this time while taking notes

4. Write down all the headlines found within the books and newsletters

5.   Write down all the headlines within the book '2001 Greatest Headlines Ever Written'

6.   Write down all the cover blurbs from an unspecified number of National Enquirer and Cosmopolitan magazine covers

7.   Write down each note you took onto a separate index card

8.   Write down each headline you copied onto a separate index card

9.   Shuffle through the index cards as you brainstorm a new promotion for your product

With these accumulated index cards, you'd have a powerful collection of ideas and headlines that have sold well in the past. And the power of these ideas will never change because we don't change.

The words may change, but the selling ideas beneath the words never change, because human nature doesn't change.

That's what Robert Collier wrote in his book 'The Robert Collier letter book.'

Now, to address the elephant in the room: most people don't complete the challenge.

In fact, I've scoured the internet and have yet to find evidence of someone completing it... exactly as prescribed by Gary.

There are 30+ page threads on forums and even a few blogs that all tried to document their progress. So far, not a single one of those posters or bloggers had finished it. At best they got about halfway. Some even deleted the blog posts of their limited progress, though they shouldn't feel too bad.

I've done it myself. I've completed it, as directed, to the letter. It just took a long, long time...

It was advertised as 30 days. But in my experience, it took nine months and one week.

That was broken down into four months of screwing around and not doing it Gary's way. Four more months of consistent daily progress doing it Gary's way. Then five weeks of 10 to 14-hour days blasting through to the finish.

That's why I don't recommend doing the 30-day challenge if you want to become a better copywriter. "Better than anyone you could hire" in Gary's words. Because it's too long and forces out almost everyone who attempts it.

And that's understandable since they expected it to take 30 days. That might not even be possible with a copious amount of illegal stimulants and a literal gun to the head.

Though there is another way...

And this is the path many of the most successful copywriters and marketers of our day have gotten an education as effective as the challenge.

This is their secret:

They took away the 30-day constraint, and read those books and hand-copied appropriate ads & headlines over the years as needed. That's how they did it.

And that's what I recommend you do too.

Focus on your current projects. Whether it's in content marketing, online advertising, affiliate marketing, lead generation, or whatever. Then leave a little bit of spare time each day or each week dedicated to reading through each book Gary recommended.

Then when you're finished, dedicate that same time to hand-copying proven headlines and ads related to your product. And over the years, reread those books to discover new insights and make new connections you were unable to make on the first read-through.

The first step to becoming a better copywriter is to find something to write. Find a way to write every day. It could be writing blog articles, testing different Facebook ads to a landing page, writing daily emails to a list, etc.

Applying your craft daily combined with gradually reading through the challenge books will super-charge your marketing ability. It will make you a better marketer than "anyone you could hire."

Daily writing will do more for you than any copywriting course could ever do.

That's because it makes you appreciate anything you learn about copywriting. As you write more and more, you start to wonder "what would be the best way to phrase this headline?" or "which benefit has greater appeal to my market?" And many more questions.

Those questions will help fuel your desire to learn more from the challenge materials over the years to come. Then you can dive in and read up on these selling ideas from the past. They'll give you further selling ammunition, experience, and perspective.

CHAPTER SIXTEEN

How can sales experience make you a better copywriter?

Going back to Gary Halbert, he once talked about two of the best ways to further improve your skill at writing copy that sells. One way was to hand-copy proven sales letters. But an even more effective way of getting better was to get real-world sales experience.

That could be door-to-door sales.

Or selling over the phone.

Or even retail sales.

Getting real sales experience is one of the most effective ways to make yourself a better copywriter.

Even the great advertiser David Ogilvy mentioned this. He was describing great copywriters of the past in his book 'Ogilvy on Advertising.' He noted many advertising greats had some form of sales experience.

And Ogilvy believed one of the reasons this helped so much was it introduced a time element into the sale. For instance, you might only have seconds to convince someone to listen to your proposal before they slam the door in your face or hang up the phone.

This appreciation for time allows you to understand at a deep level how important it is to quickly capture someone's attention and interest. Before they decide to move on to something else.

So before their prospect hung up the phone or before they slammed the door in their face... There was a certain amount of time the salesperson had before that prospect shut them out of the sale.

This conditioned them to learn how to make the most of that initial time. And that helped them craft powerful attention-grabbing headlines and leads. That helped capture the interest of the target market right away and hold them all the way down the greased sales slide.

That's one of the reasons why real sales experience is one of the most powerful ways to improve your copy. It was common among some of the best copywriters of all time.

And Ogilvy also noticed copywriters who hand-copy promotions from the past also tend to do well. So those are two proven ways to become a master copywriter.

Top copywriters have recommended them (and practiced them) over the years.

CHAPTER SEVENTEEN

Conclusion

Congratulations! You've made it to the end of the book. Usually, only around 5% of readers actually read books all the way (and from a study of Kindle readers, only 59% even opened the books they bought).

You're one of the top 5% of readers. That's something you can feel proud of.

Throughout this book, we've talked about various copywriting guidelines, selling ideas, target markets, business arithmetic, and research.

Going forward, make sure you take action to improve your copywriting ability. Do this by both sticking to the basic copywriting & business guidelines from throughout this book. And also read some of the great copywriting books of the past to get an appreciation for the source material.

If you found this book helpful and want to further improve your copywriting and marketing skills, then go to my website. Check out more of my related books, courses, and services on FraserDruet.com

Recommended Copywriting Authorities

Here is a list of copywriting-related authorities I'm fond of. I'd recommend seeking out and devouring every single book, course, newsletter, article, sales material, and interview you can find of theirs. Consume them multiple times if you're up for it. Some of these authorities have even read books of their peers over 60 times (and they found the last 20 readings to be the most beneficial).

There are some great marketers I've left out who are more platform-specific, and others who I haven't had the pleasure of reading yet, but these are at least ones I've read and can vouch for.

- Gary Halbert
- Gary Bencivenga
- John Carlton
- Dan Kennedy
- Jay Abraham
- Clayton Makepeace

- Joe Sugarman

- Russell Brunson

- Ben Settle

- Eugene Schwartz

- Claude Hopkins

- Robert Collier

- John Caples

- Victor Schwab

- Joe Karbo

- Ben Suarez

- Joe Cossman

- E. Haldeman-Julius

- Vincent James

- Matt Furey

- David Ogilvy

- Mark Joyner

- Maria Veloso

- Joe Polish

- Michael Masterson (pen name of Mark Ford)

- Doberman Dan

NOTES

NOTES

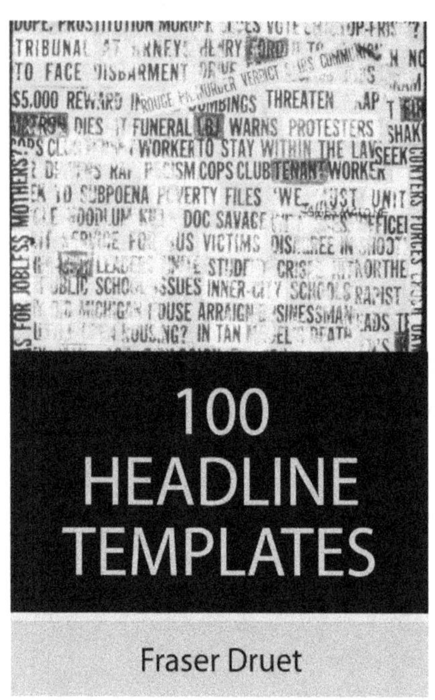

FREE

As a way of saying thank you for buying my book, here is a link to my '**100 Headline Templates**' Ebook 100% FREE!

It contains 100 simple ideas and corresponding examples you could incorporate into your headlines. Try incorporating some and test them to see which ones your market responds best to.

TO DOWNLOAD GO TO:

https://FraserDruet.com/BookDownloadBonus

www.ingramcontent.com/pod-product-compliance
Lightning Source LLC
Chambersburg PA
CBHW061053050726
47592CB00004B/1666